Reflections

Daron Kenneth

authorHOUSE®

AuthorHouse™
1663 Liberty Drive
Bloomington, IN 47403
www.authorhouse.com
Phone: 1-800-839-8640

Published by AuthorHouse 9/24/12

ISBN: 978-1-4772-7428-6 (sc)
ISBN: 978-1-4772-7427-9 (dj)
ISBN: 978-1-4772-7426-2 (e)

Library of Congress Control Number: 2012917826

Any people depicted in stock imagery provided by Thinkstock are models, and such images are being used for illustrative purposes only. Certain stock imagery © Thinkstock.

This book is printed on acid-free paper.

Because of the dynamic nature of the Internet, any web addresses or links contained in this book may have changed since publication and may no longer be valid. The views expressed in this work are solely those of the author and do not necessarily reflect the views of the publisher, and the publisher hereby disclaims any responsibility for them.

A Walk in the City

There's nothing as special as a walk in the city, just
Holding hands with the one I Love. While walking
You can feel the pace of each other as we walk along
The city sidewalks and roads. Once in a while I feel
Your hand squeeze a pulse of energy as we continue
Our walking. Your hand warms my hand as we walk
Throughout the neighborhood, just you and me, just
You and me, just you and me walking along on the
Sidewalk on a brisk fall day. SomeTymes we raise
Our hands to wave "Hello" to some friends and then it's
Back to our walk. The cool, fall air is crisp and stark
So we pick up the pace to keep our body's temperature
As warm as our two hands clutched together. When
We get to the park, we stop for a moment's rest on
One of the benches. The sounds of the kids playing
Reminds us of when we were younger so many years
Ago. We sit side by side with our hands clasped and
Discuss the changing weather and realize full well
That soon winter will be here and it will be too cold
For walking to the park, so we just try to take in all
Of the beauty of fall that nature has to offer us. We
Get up and realize that it will be dark soon, so we
Just continue our walk homeward just enjoying each
Other's company and walk in the leaves and listen
To their crunching sounds as we slowly find our way
Back home.

1

All By Myself

All alone and by myself I sit and listen to the Spring
Breeze blow by. I hear the sound of the air as she
Moves through the trees blowing softly. I hear
The sound of the wind as she blows gently across
The lawn making the leaves of grass blow to and fro
As she warms the ground with her warm, gentle air.
Up in the trees the leaves on the branches move back
And forth and they dance in her air as she sets them
In motion. Sitting on a chair in the middle of it all
I smell the scent of freshly cut lawns and the soft
Scent of lilacs in the air. I smell the sweet scent
Of cherry blossoms blooming in her pockets of air
As she sends the sweet aroma high up into the air.
Small bees dance around in the breeze carrying the
Pollen from flower to flower. Because it is such a
Nice day you can hear the sound of children's
Laughter as they play at a nearby park. Some young
People are playing basketball and you can hear them
Chiding in unison as they score a point or two. The
Best part of all is the sight of a couple walking merrily
Through the neighborhood and holding hands as they
Just walk on by in the gentle breezes. Taking it all in
Is a picturesque view of life moving as slowly and as
Gently as the breezes herself.

All For You

Every day is special because of you. You
Help to bring a smile to my face. Your
Good natured demeanor always puts me
In a great mood. I can't help but be
Reminded of all the wonderful things
That you do for me. I do so very much
Enjoy spending Tyme with you because
When we spend Tyme together we always
Have an wonderful Tyme. Your kindness
Is one of the many reasons that I like to
Spend Tyme with you as well. Whether
It is going to dinner or a movie or just
Spending some Tyme together at home,
You make each moment special and
Memorable. It reminds me how lucky
I am to have found my best friend and
Loved one all in the same person. I am
Truly blessed to have found my true Love
In you.

All of You

Your smile, so warm and true, brings a smile
To my face whenever it is that I think of you
And all the nice things that you do to make
My day special and unique. Your eyes, like
A window to your soul, say hello and smile
Back at me whenever it is that I see them
Looking at me and sharing a special moment.
Your heart, so warm and true shares in the
Acts of kindness that you share with me in
Each and everything you do for me. Your
Arms, when outstretched are like an exten-
Sion of yourself. They help to remind me
Just how truly wonderful it is to hold your
Hand in my hand or you in my arms when they
Are holding on to you. Your soul is beautiful
As you are. Your acts of kindness help to
Make the world a much better place to live.
Your soul helps spread joy in the world and
Make it a more peaceful place. All of these
Together make up the totality of you, that
Special someone who I so enjoy spending Tyme with.

Always

The next Tyme that you feel old,
Or need a hand to hold,
Baby, turn to me,
Darling, then you'll see,
We were always meant to be.

The next Tyme you're alone,
With nowhere else to go,
Baby turn to me,
Darling then you'll see
We were always meant to be.

The next Tyme that you're down,
And stuck wearing a frown,
Baby, turn to me,
Daring, then you'll see,
We were always meant to be.

The next Tyme you feel sad,
Or the world's left you mad,
Baby, turn to me,
Darling, then you'll see,
We were always meant to be.

The next Tyme you feel unhappy,
Or you're feeling crappy,
Baby, turn to me,
Darling, then you'll see,
We were always meant to be…ALWAYS.

Beaches

When the sun shines over the ocean, there's a feeling
That you get deep inside. It's something in the way
That the water sparkles that gives you a feeling of
Elation. When the water breaks on the beach, it fills
You with a feeling of pure peace. There's something
About the way it sounds that gives you a natural form
Of relaxation. It is something that you just can't find
Anywhere else in nature…anywhere else indeed. The
Sound of the waves crashing on the shore gives you
A feeling that says, "Stop what you're doing and just
Sit down here for a while and listen to the sounds of
Nature, and everything else will fall into place."
There's the smell of the sea water, that salty scent that
Works magic on your soul…fresh…clean and pure.
The sights, sounds, and smells of the ocean that helps
Put all that stress to rest. If by chance you happen to
Find a nice big seashell on the beach, it gives you
Your own mini beach to take home with you, along
With a reminder of the sounds that you hear when
You place it next to your ears that says, "Slow down
And relax and let the sounds of the beach fix what
Ails you."

Cat Tyme

When I'm feeling down and out I seek your quirky
Smile and however that I'm feeling disappears for
Just a while.

When I'm feeling sad I seek your furry face and
However that I'm feeling disappears without a
Trace.

When I'm feeling lonely I seek your eyes of blue
And however that I'm feeling will end when I'm With you.

When I'm feeling frightened I seek to hold you
Now and however that I'm feeling will disappear
Some how.

When I'm feeling angry I seek to hold you when
You're free and however that I'm feeling you'll
Fill my heart with glee.

When I'm feeling happy I seek to hold you on my
Lap and however that I'm feeling you'll help to
Make me laugh.

Celebrate

When you're with me and the daylight comes
I know just how lucky I am…for every day's
Like my birthday and each night is just like
Christmas Eve because when we're together
Every day gets a little bit better than the one
That I had before it. Every day's just like
Valentine's and every Sunday's just like Easter,
Just another day to celebrate the fact that
We're together, the fact that we're still in Love.
The days roll by sequentially in Tyme, but each
Day's a holiday, for when I wake up in your
Arms, I can't help but celebrate a little bit more.
Special days, special days, each day is special
Now for when I get to hold you close it is a
Day that can't go by without some recognition.
When every day's your birthday and each night
Like Christmas Eve, I know I've found the right
One to Love, so celebrate with me.

Chasing Sleep

When I get down and so tired that I can't see
Straight, all I want to do is to sleep some more.
Nothing else matters except trying to conserve
My energy any way that I can. I can get so
Tired that even breathing feels like it is taking
Up all of my energy. I spend my Tyme sleeping
To get caught up, but when I wake up, I still
Want more sleep. That's the way I spend most
Of my Tyme …chasing sleep. If I close my eyes
For even a moment I find that I am nodding off
To sleep once more. Sleep is my friend. When
I don't have enough energy to do anything else
I know that if I lay my head down I will find
Sleep. When there's nothing else that makes
Any sense to try, I know sleep will always come To me.
Sleeping is my favorite pasTyme when
I am feeling low because it is the only thing I
Can do when I am exhausted and needing to
Store up what little energy I can muster up.
Sleeping helps to pass the Tyme when I am
Down and it will be the constant "friend" that
Serves me while I am feeling low.

Couch Tyme

SomeTymes when I'm all alone
I'll sit upon the couch and stretch
My arms and legs out till they can
Stretch no more. Then I cuddle
Up with a cat and just spend my
Tyme brushing and petting the one
I Love so well. I like to stroke her
Fur and brush her face and then just
Listen as she purrs. I Love to watch
Her spend Tyme rolling in ecstasy
As I rub her belly and scratch her
Ears and kiss her on the forehead.
When I look into her eyes I some-
Tymes see a sadness that tells me
She is unhappy with being a house
Cat and not one that is able to run
Outdoors like some of her wilder
Cousins. I know that she couldn't
Survive outside on her own and so
The dilemma remains: to let her have
Her own space indoors or to let her
Run free. I know that if she isn't
Completely content to live indoors,
She is all the safer and better off for
It. So now it's back to lounging on
The couch as we take a nap together

Crawl

If I could crawl back in Tyme
I'd make my life sublime,
Then I'd set my soul free
The way I used to be:
FREE...FREE...FREE...

I used to be young
I had lots of fun,
Now nothing's now new
What's this boy supposed to do
When he's lost his soul
And can't fight my way back,
Now it's the freedom I lack.

Please let me be free
Please let me be free,
Please set my soul free.

It feels like a hand's got a hold
And grasping hard at my soul,
Pulling me down to the ground
Pulling my weight all around
DOWN...DOWN...DOWN...

Nothing can set my soul free
Nothing's going to let me be me
No, I can't fight my way back
Because it's the freedom I lack
Please let me be free
Set my soul FREE
Set my soul FREE...FREE...FREE

Dark Afternoon

It's a dark afternoon and I'm all alone just trying
To find the doorway to the peace that I seek. Peace
Won't come so I pray I will find a way home to the
Peace I seek, some how, some way, some where.
The dark surrounds me, every where I turn and all
I can do is falter through it once more and I do, I do
Yes I do. The afternoon has turned to night and I'm
Still all alone. I'm still looking for that door to the
Peace that I seek, but it won't come, no it still won't
Come. I'm stuck here treading water in the darkness
Everywhere. The darkness surrounds me, envelops
Me, as my mind just prays for freedom. I search to
Find the light I seek out there, somewhere. So I
Pray, yes I pray, I still pray, yet the light I seek evades
Me as I stumble through the darkness. I'm still
Searching to find the right way to turn. When morn-
Ing finally comes and the rays of light shine through
I just thank the heavens above for letting me make it
Through another day of many in the dark.

Darkness Falls

As I walk down the streets of this evening
I walk alone throughout the darkness…
And should I stop to meet up with someone
It would be apparent through the portals
That are mine eyes that I am filled with
Sadness…A sadness that follows everywhere
That I turn. No there is no white light that
Envelops me or follows in my footsteps.
Darkness falls on the path that I tread and
Fills my heart with melancholy. Never to
Be anything but morose, I step heavy and
Carry my heart in my hands as if it were an
Object that had only served me to beat in a
Chorus that keeps in Tyme with the soul of
My depression as darkness is my only friend.

Day After Day

Day after day the sun rises and then sets. With
Each day is a new beginning and ending. And
With each day is another chance to find your
Own new meaning and resolve the old ways
That don't work any more. Tyme brings many
Changes, but changes don't come easy because
We get set in our ways of doing things, even if
They aren't the best things for us to choose.
Tyme is the constant that we all share, because
Tyme is the only factor that is constant to all
Of our choices we make. Tyme continues to
Move forward even if we get stuck moving in
Reverse and can't find the reason for making
A change that we need to make. Tyme keeps
Moving forward and with each day we only
Get older and perhaps a bit wiser as we make
Small efforts to become the person we could
Be, the person we should be, the person we
Were meant to be.

Down In a Hole

Feels like I'm down in a hole
Feels like I can't find my soul,
Nothing's familiar anymore
Can't find my way to the door,
I need to fight my way back to what's real
I need to fight for the things that I feel,
You leave me here feeling all alone
Just sitting here all alone by the phone,
Nothing hurts more than to know
That this is the end of the road,
All alone,
All alone,
   All alone over you.

So now I'm alone and it's true
The only one I miss is you,
You brought me back from my past
You made me feel alive at last,
Oh, can't you see that I'm here in pain
Hoping for you to come back here again,
You made my whole world to shine
You made me smile every Tyme,
Nothing hurts more than to know
That this is the end of the road,
I'm all alone,
 All alone,
  All alone over you.

No nothing hurts more than to know
That this is the end of the road,
All I can do now is let go
Let go...Let go...Let go...
I have to let go of you.

Fade Away

Once we were good friends
But now you're on your own,
Friendships shouldn't end
Now I'm left here all alone.

When I look at you
I start to fade away,
It leaves me here quite sad
There's nothing more to say.

I think about you often
Like friends will someTymes
Do, you're nowhere to be found
It leaves me here quite blue.

I miss our talking mostly
Those calls got me through the day,
But now I'm left here lonely
As your memories slowly fade.

Someday it will happen to you
You'll miss our friendship true,
You'll find you wish that I was there
You'll find you miss me too

Faith

When I was a little boy
I had so much faith in the world,
Nothing could change how I felt
Yes, I had so much faith in the world.

But when I got a little older
It just seemed life was growing colder,
Life wasn't all that it seemed
Life was more like a dream.

Now I never feel like I fit in
I was chasing dreams once again,
Friends weren't as kind as they seemed
Friends were just like a dream,
All fading fast, fading fast, fading fast.

So now I hold on to my dreams once again
As I remember the places I've been,
Some day I hope that I'll find
A little bit more of my mind,
Just a little bit more of my mind.

All I can remember is the past
It's just fading fast, so fast, fading fast,
So I'll hold onto my memories of you
The only thing in my heart that rings true,
So I'll hold onto my memories of you
The only thing in my heart that rings true,
It's YOU...
IT'S YOU...
IT'S YOU...

Falling Down Deep

I'm falling, yes I'm falling into the dark. I fall
Deeper, and deeper into the dark. I can feel my
Energies dwindling away. I don't know which
Way to turn to find solace from the darkness
That surrounds me. I just seek the light of peace
That will lift my spirits up and keep my mind
Off of the edge. Nothing that I say or do will
Help me turn away from the darkness all around
Me. So I fall deeper into the dark and fall even
Further from the light. I'm falling, yes I'm
Falling, I just keep falling deeper into the dark.
While I fall I turn and shout to find the help I
Seek to find. Somewhere, hiding, somewhere
There must be some help. As I fall I seek to
Call on what little energies I still retain. But
All I can do is fall deeper and farther into this
Hole that I'm in. So now I scream for help, but
Help won't come, so I'm left here on my own.
Falling, still falling into this hell that holds me
Fast. Deeper, darker, farther into this pit of
Abyss. When I finally hit the bottom I realize
That I can go no further and I'm stuck here
Climbing my way out of this pit I'm in. And
Somehow, someway I will find redemption
From the darkness, somewhere, somehow,
Someway, but when?

Father, Father

Father, father, can you hear me? I'm down
Here below. And from Tyme to Tyme I look
Up at the sky and wonder if you see me down
Here staring up at you in the sky. I wonder
Can you hear me, can you see me and do you
Care? Your Tyme is now done down here below,
But I know you linger on in the heavens above.
Are you cold? Are you lonely? What are you
Feeling today? Today? Today? Do you know
How much I still miss you? Do you know?
Does it even matter any way? And if you're
Listening, what are you thinking of the world
You left behind down here below? Do you
Miss all that you left behind? Do you miss
Those that you left behind? Are you singing
With grandma today? Today?

Feeling Down

When I'm down and feeling low
I know exactly what to do,
I close my eyes and then I know,
And I don't have to feel low anymore.

When I'm down and feeling mad
I know exactly what to do,
I close my eyes and then I'm glad,
And I don't have to feel mad anymore.

When I'm down and feeling uptight
I know exactly what to do,
I close my eyes and then I'm alright,
And I don't have to feel uptight anymore.

When I'm down and feeling alone
I know exactly what to do,
I close my eyes and I'm in another zone,
And I don't have to feel alone anymore.

Footprints

We walked to the sea, just waiting for tide
To come in. After that we watched so very
Patiently for the moon to have her way with
The water's edge. While the moon worked
On the water, we dashed about in the cool,
Wet water. We were not really swimming,
But wading in and out of the water so as to
Cool us down on this very hot day. Kicking
The water up and splashing around, just
Acting like we were a couple of kids, we
Had the Tyme of our lives. We were just
Laughing like crazy and taking it all in.
We made a castle out of wet sand and then
Watched the water slowly rise and wash it
All away. We stalked the water's edge for
Shells to take home with us as a souvenir
Of our little trip to the beach. We sat along
The coast of the bay drawing pictures in the
Sand and when all was said and done we left
The water behind us with nothing as proof
That we had been there buy some footprints
In the sand.

For My Mother

You are my mother, and yet you are so much
More. You are the person that I confide in.
You are the person that I Love to spend Tyme
With when we're together. You are the reason
That I am here, for without you, I literally never
Would have been born. We share conversations
And secrets that I can't share with others because
You always give me your honest opinion and
You don't pass judgment on me. You also want
What's best for me and you tell me so. Even
Though we may disagree from Tyme to Tyme
I know we will always be connected by blood.
Likewise I want you to be happy because you
Are such an important part of my life and you
Always will be because we share a sacred mother
And son bond. You always have kind things to
Say and I hope that I can in return say the things
That will help to make each and every day as Special for you.

For My Sister

You are such an important part of my life.
We are now being joined together spiritually
In a way that has been in the past elusive to
Us. I know that when we were younger, we
Were so very close and then as someTymes
Happens, we grew far apart for what seemed
Like an eternity. But now, thanks to good
Communication, our brother and sister bond
Has grown strong again. I fondly remember
Our years together as children and how very
Close we were way back then. I'm glad our
Lines of communication have grown stronger
As of lately because I so enjoy talking to you
Once again. I know that we are extremely
Different people now than we were oh, so
many years ago as children. I also know that
These differences are what make our conver-
Sations so much more interesting now when
We do talk. I look forward to many, many
More years of sharing our Tyme and our
Conversations together. I am so glad that
We are friends once again.

Forevermore

I am but a dreamer who lives here in this
Shell that was once a soul. Trying to
Move forward, but always moving in
Reverse more than ahead. I try not to
Live in the past but it is what I do best.
I go to bed at night and dream away the
Hours, hoping for success when I waken
But never to see it come to fruition. I
Live in my dream world just waiting for
All to come to pass as I hoped it would,
As I know it could, as I hoped it should.
But as they say, careful what you wish
For…you just might get your dream to
Come true, but not exactly as you thought
It would be. But then again, you just might
Be everything that you wished for and more.
So I just sit here waiting patiently for that
Moment to arrive in Tyme. And so I wait…
And I wait…and I wait some more…
Waiting now forevermore.

Her Little World

She sits so sad and lonely, just wondering
What she has to do to make a change and
Not be all alone. She picks up a big piece
Of chalk and goes out to the sidewalk and
Begins to sketch out a picture of the way
She wishes it could be: some nice shoes,
A fancy dress, and a necklace around her
Slender neck. Maybe it is made of rare
Stones or maybe made of pearls. Either
Way, she knows its just a fantasy, it is
Something that she'll probably see in this
LifeTyme. She continues on with a great
Big house and a car parked out in front of
Her imaginary world that she has made for
Herself. As she finishes she looks at the
World she really lives in: worn out shoes
That someone couldn't fit into any more,
A tattered outfit of clothes and a bracelet
From the dollar store. As she finishes her
Drawing of her imaginary, would be world
She hears a voice calling out to her. It is
Her mother reminding her to come in for
Dinner. As she walks up the stairs to her
Front door, she realizes that she may not
Have all that she wants, but her world is
Full of the Love of her mother and sisters
And for now that suits her just fine.

I Can Count On You

When days get long and Tymes get tough,
It's always nice to know that I can count
On you to be there for me and when I need
A shoulder to lean on. When I am feeling
Down or feeling sad, you are always there
For me with kind words to say and support
For me. You always have that special way
Of always saying just the right thing at just
The right Tyme. You always offer your
Advice and an outstretched pair of arms to
hold me when it is what I need most. I
Know that I can count on you to be there to
Hold me up when life has gotten me down
And a hug when the right Tyme presents
Itself. But more, much more than this, you
Always have a hand to hold when the Tyme
Is right.

I Just Say Your Name

So now I wake and think of you and there's
Nothing that I'd rather be doing, and when
I do a smile crosses my face when I remember
The kiss that you gave me last night before we
Went to sleep. Then I recall the words that
You said to me and I can't help but smile once
Again. You're always there to remind me
Just how lucky that I am to have found my
Perfect soul mate in you. As I make my way
Through my day, I am so glad that I found
You and made you a part of my life, so I
Remind myself here and there just what a
Wonderful pair we make, you and I, just us
And I can't help but smile some more. If
Anyone asks me why I'm smiling I just
Smile and say your name.

I Love You...

I Love you because...you make me smile.
I Love you because...you are so gentle.
I Love you because...you are so kind.
I Love you because...you are so smart.
I Love you because...you are so handsome.
I Love you because...you are such a good friend.
I Love you because...you cuddle with me.
I Love you because...you are so sensible.
I Love you so much it's incomprehensible.
I Love you because...you are YOU!!

I Must Be Dreaming

You, you are the one that I Love so much. You
Are the one that I Love so easily. You just place
Your hand in mine and I get lost in Tyme. I am
So Lost without you. I feel your body heat so
Warm and so wonderful...am I dreaming? Your
Body is so close, so very close to mine that I
Swear I must be dreaming. Never in this world
Have I Loved someone so much. Magic, yes it
Feels like magic as we lay here next to one
Another. I don't ever want to lose this feeling
That I'm feeling when you're here and you're
All mine. I'm trapped here in a snippet of Tyme.
Please don't ever leave my side. Now that we
Are here the emotions run full clear that we are
One together. One heart, one mind and one soul.
Now that we are here, I know that I have found
My purpose in life and that is to make you happy
Too. So take your arms and place them around
Me and just give me a kiss that reminds me too
That you Love me, yes you really Love me as
Much as I Love you.

I Turn to You

If I'm feeling alone there's one place I can
Turn to make me feel whole again, that's
You. You make my life livable, even if it's
Just you and me together. When I'm feeling
Stranded in the dark of night and there seems
To be no help anywhere, I turn to you to be
My beacon and give me the help I need to
Find my way home. When life can bring me
Down and there seems to be nothing I can do
To lift my spirits, I turn to you and you're
The support that I need to help me realize
There's nothing more I need than you to be
The one by my side to lift my emotions up-
Wards. When I'm tired and feeling like I've
Lost the energy to keep going, I know that
I can always count on you to be there for me
To lean on while I'm waiting for my soul to
Replenish itself. I know you'll be the company
Through the Tymes while I'm waiting for
That to happen.

I Wonder...

When it's late at night and I can't sleep
I find myself thinking about the past
And I wonder to myself how things
Could've been different all of those
Years ago. I wonder what would've
Happened had my father not been an
Alcoholic that he was. What kind of
Difference it would have on my life
And the life of my family? What kind
Of life would we have had together?
Would it have been better or worse?
Then I get to thinking just what it
Would've been like to live a life free
Of depression and manic episodes.
Would I still be me? Would I have
Been a better person? And more
Importantly, would I be a happier
Person than the one I am with the
Things being the way that they are?
And what about my family, what
Would I be like without my mother
And my sister? Would I be as nice
And as kind of a person or would I
Be totally different from the soul that
I am? I am also curious as to what
Kind of friend I would be to others
If I didn't have the same set of parents
That I was born with. I wonder, yes
I wonder...yes I do.

On Darkness

I am truly a soul that lives in darkness.
And though I pass the souls of others
That reflect the light, I follow along
And I try to retain enough of that
Brightness as to reveal the path of
The road that I tread so as not to walk
On blindly through this causeway
Without some form of direction or
Path of truth as to where I go. As I
Walk on I choose to follow in the
Paths of others so as to have some
Light to shine on the path of darkness
That I tread. For the truth be known
The only route that I travel is surely
As dark as the deepest pits of hell
On earth.

In Dreams

When the evening comes, I find myself
Trying to catch some sleep…but sleep
Does not come so easily, so I lay down
And find that the bed upon which I sleep
Is the only one that I can depend upon
To ease my mind and allow slumber to
Come at last. When I am finally asleep
It is with a heavy heart that the dreams
That do come to me are filled with as
Much darkness as the dayTyme hours
That I live in. Deep, dark, and twisted
Dreams haunt me in the day as well as
The night…for when I wake from these
Dreams I am so frightened that often I
Cannot fall back to sleep. I am often
Shaken awake with the sheer force that
One hits a wall in a fit of drunken abyss.
The dreams I have can only be described
As demented, demonic and horrific. They
Follow me throughout my sleep as well
As my wakened hours and cause me to
Feel as though my mind were not mine
Own and under sinister control as to
Leave me frightened and in fear of my
Nights as well as my days…in fear of
My nights as well as my days…in fear
Of my nights as well as my days.

In My Room

When I'm feeling down, I step into my room,
A place where I am free to feel safe and alone.
And when the world is making me low, there's
Just one place where I go to…my room. it's a
Place where the music is always on and it's a
Place where I feel safe and sound and when no
One else is around I'm free to be myself.
When I was young I used to go to my favorite
Place by a waterfall and it always helped to
Cure my bad moods. But now I'm older and
That waterfall is miles and miles away from
Me. I often think back to those younger days
So very far away and just how very much they
Meant to me, those hours on my own. Now
When I need some space from the world I
Retreat to my room and remember just how
Very nice it feels to escape this world from
Tyme to Tyme. Outside in the world all my
Problems seem to overwhelm me, but here
In my room it's just me and my four walls
And some softly playing music. The rest
Of the world seems miles away and all I can
Do is sit back and enjoy the peaceful place
That I'm in. Serenity and peace overrule all
Of the bad things in the world and it's nice
To have a place to call my own.

On the Sun

In the sun, in the sun, I used to play in the sun
All throughout my days when I was young. I
Prayed those days would never end, oh, how
I prayed those days would never end. As I
Got older and so much wiser I found that I
Was busy doing those things that young men
Do. As I grew I grew up knowing that the
Sun was my best friend. I spent my Tyme
Without an end just chasing those rays of
Gold from the heavens above. I went to the
Beach and then I swam for what seemed like
An eternity, then I just sat on the shoreline
Tanning some more. As I grew older, the
World grew colder and I longed for those
Days of old when I was young. Back when
I was young I grew and really changed my
Life. I had so many things I had to do, so
Many things to do. But as I grew I kept my
Memories of that young boy in the sun.
Now that I am older, so much older all the
Things I do can't keep me from the place I
Long to be, out on the shoreline catching
Rays and a breeze from the sand and sea.

Just a Little Bit More

I feel your body near me, so close to mine.
The touch of your skin helps to warm me
On a winter's day as you ease your body
Closer so I can whisper in your ear how
Much I Love you and how much I treasure
Your kindness. You turn your head to
Listen to my words and smile a great big
Smile as you hear what I have to say. We
Are so close, us too, that we have to but
Merely breathe the words that you hear
From me to you. Your eyes glance at me
And send me a message that you feel the
Same way that I do. I stare deep into the
Darkness of your eyes and see my reflection
In them. Your eyes, so deep and dark are
Beautiful and warm. I ask you if you Love
Me and your smile answers back to me a
Definite "Yes". I take your hand in mine
And hold it tenderly, so tenderly that you
Whisper back to me that you are in Love
With me too. I hold you in a warm embrace
Until I can hold you no more. Then I kiss
You and Love until we are both spent of
Our energies. Then I Love you just a little
Bit more…a little bit more…just a little bit
More.

Just Being You

When I wake in the morning sun, I
Long to see your face returning a
Smile to me. Even though you are
Far away now, the fact that you might
Be thinking the very same thing, brings
A smile to my face anyway. Your
Smiling face, your bright eyes and
Your wonderful sense of humor all
Come together to make up the reasons
That I fell in Love with you in the
First place so many years ago. They
Remain the same reasons that I still
Love you after all these years. Even
If we can't be together right now, I
Know that I'll soon have you back
In my arms. To have and to hold you
Is the greatest gift I could have ever
Received in my lifeTyme. You are
The reason that I wake in the morning.
You are the reason that I smile during
The day, and you are the reason that
When we fall asleep together at night
That I can rest easy. Thank you for
Being the reason that I live and breathe.
Thank you for just being you.

Just Imagine It

Our world is a bold and stark place
Where people from all different
Races and places meld into one
Big giant group of ideas, hopes
And dreams. A place where we
All try to live and survive the
State of affairs that has brought
Us together. A place where the
Individual can interact and
Learn from all of the others that
Are around them. A place where
We can share different forms of
Religious, political and social
Views and yet all interact despite
Our differences. If we could all
Just learn to treat each other like
We were all members of the same
Family we could all get along so
Much better. It is possible to end
All of the warring and fighting if
We all kept our minds open to the
Possibility. If we all just got along
Think what more we could learn
From one another…and what an
Amazing thing that would be…
Just imagine it.

Just You

You, you make my dreams come true. With
Each and everything we do together, I am
Reminded just what a wonderful person
That you are. Your acts of kindness tell
Me that you are a truly great soul. Your
Smile brings a smile to my face. Each and
Every day I am reminded how kind you are.
You are always doing nice things for me
Because that's just the kind of person that
You are. Your warm heart is shared in each
And everything that you do for myself as
Well as others. Your eyes say, "Hello" and
Offer a smile. They make me feel happy and
Truly blessed to have found you for a
Friend as well as my Lover.

Keep Searching

Once when I was much younger and I was
So all alone, I didn't have anybody or any-
Thing or any place to call home. I used to
Walk around town searching for some place
To call mine own. I'd walk around alone,
(believe me there's nothing worse than being
Alone). Oh, but I grew wiser, just knowing
That my special someone and special place
Were out there I'd just have to keep looking
And keep searching for someone to call my
Own. Keep looking and one day at a Tyme,
If you never give up you will find your own
Special someone and that place where you
Fit in. Don't give up or never give in until
You find that special someone and your own
Place in the sun. It's out there and they are
Just waiting for a chance to find you too.

Lap Cat

Her nose is wet and cool
Her paws are warm and soft,
Her fur is dark and gray
SomeTymes she acts aloft.

SomeTymes she sits and yawns
While her tail moves from side to side,
Her eyes are a beautiful green
She smiles so nice and bright.

She always seems so mellow
SomeTymes she looks so sad,
You can always pet her
Except for when she's mad.

She has a nice demeanor
She likes to give me a kiss,
She likes to roll in catnip
Till she's in a state of bliss.

She acts quite regally as
She marches through the house,
She'll creep into the basement
While searching for a mouse.

She'll sit upon my lap
Then she'll stare into my eyes,
SomeTymes she looks so lonely
I'd like to change her mind.

Late in the Night

SomeTymes when it is night and I can't find
Sleep, I spend my Tyme just reiterating all
Of the wonderful things that make up you.
I am never at a loss to be reminded of all
The wonderful things that you do each and
Every day to help make the lives of those
With whom you interact a more special
Place in which to live. When I am sleepless
I bring to mind all of the things that make
Me Love you just for you: your smile, your
Eyes, your warm heart, your outstretched
Arms and your soul. Each of these things
Helps to make you uniquely you. Your
Kindness and your generosity speak volumes
About what kind of person that you are.
You are always giving of yourself. Something
Truly rare and hard to come by these days.
Don't ever change the way you are. It is "you"
In yourself that I so adore and long to spend
The rest of my life with.

Let the Sun Shine

Let the sun shine into your eyes,
Let the sun shine down on you,
Let the sun shine into your eyes,
Let the sun shine down on you.

The sun is shining for a little while,
The sun is shining it will make you smile,
The sun is shining on the world today,
The sun is shining let's go out and play.

And when the sun shine into your eyes,
And when the sun shine down on you,
And when the sun shine into your eyes,
And when the sun shine down on you.

The sun is shining so don't feel bad,
The sun is shining so don't feel sad,
The sun is shining so don't turn away,
The sun is shining so here's what I say.

So when the sun shines into your eyes,
So when the sun shines down on you,
So when the sun shines into your eyes,
So when the sun shines down on you.

The sun is shining so don't feel down,
The sun is shining so let it shine all around,
The sun is shining so don't feel blue,
The sun is shining so let yourself feel anew.

Life Without You

Right now my life feels so strange
Kind of like my mind's been rearranged,
Can't fight back these memories of you
Got to fight my way back to the truth.

You were always the one who was there
You always showed that you cared,
But now something has gone quite wrong
We can't even seem to just get along.

Now you've gone and made life a mess
You're really no better than the rest,
You went and found someone new
Now you leave me here feeling so blue.

Still I'm here clinging on to the past
Now it's leaving me here fading fast,
All I wanted was nothing but you
Now you leave me here feeling so blue.

What I must now do is let go
Now I need to leave you there all alone,
I must rely on myself once again
I must cut my ties with you my friend.

I was once standing so strong
But living without you is just wrong,
I know I'm the one who is right
All you do is just put up a fight.

What I must do is now let you go
This just leaves me here all alone,
I must rely on myself once again
Next Tyme I will find a better friend.

Listen to Music

When the day grows too long or the night
Too intense, there's only one thing that
Can cushion the severity of the problem:
Music. I can't begin to explain how very
Important music is to this planet, but most
People would agree it is of paramount
Importance. It is amazing what just a few
Bars of sound can do when we are weary.
It can give us courage, it can invite us to
Dance, it can calm our nerves, it can even
Lull us to sleep when sleep will not come
To us. I find that I am prone to enjoying
Most types of music, but then again there
Are types of music that can steer our nerves
In the wrong direction. It is amazing that
On this earth there are so many styles of
Music and each with its own unique sound.
People are as unique as there are types of
Music. It is hard to understand why people
Who are basically the same genetic makeup
Choose such varying styles of music to enjoy
Especially for different reasons. Even though
We are all generally the same makeup we
Have as many reasons for choosing different
Types of music as there are emotions. One
Thing is for sure, it is hard to find anyone
Who doesn't enjoy at least one style of music
When they choose to relax and unwind. It is
True that music calms the savage beast and
Can serve as an important means of communi-
Cating our thoughts and our ideas.

Little Boy

When I was a little boy
I had some choices to make,
When I was a little boy
I had some chances to take,
But I took the road to the city
Where everything looked
So nice and so pretty.

And the world had had all it's own shine
And it helped me feel so sublime,
But now I've grown older
And the world has grown colder,
Nothing shines like before
Now everything's rotten to the core,
I should have taken the other road
I wouldn't feel so lost and so old,
I'd still have my chance to be free,
Now I'd rather hide from the things I see.

Now nothing's going to change my life
I can't go back and make her my wife,
I should have taken the other road
I wouldn't feel so lost and so old,
I'd still have my chances to be free
And not hide from the world that I see.

Now nothing's going to change my life
I can't go back…I'm here facing my strife,
I should have taken the other road
Then I wouldn't feel so lost and so old,
I'd still have my chance to be free
And not hide from the world that I see.

Lost Days

Some days are lost days. They're lost days because
You can't get them back. On lost days you don't get
Anything done except for feeling remorse for the
Things that you wanted to achieve but weren't
Successful at reaching your goals. Lost days are
Days that you can only wish for more of the things
That you wanted to do to be achieved. You feel sad
And lonely and wish for your happiness. I find that
Lost days are better spent in bed and sleeping because
As much as crying lets the flood gates open to wash
Away the pain, they don't accomplish the goals that
You have set for yourself for that day. Crying and
Feeling bad can be useful because someTymes we
Just keep on building on the pain that we're holding
In. Eventually you have to let go of the pain.Some-
Tymes I just need to let go of the rivers of tears and
Face all the upset that lies behind all of the pain.
Pain and anguish seem to go hand in hand and the
Release that you get from crying can be good for the
Soul. Sleeping through a lost day seems more like
Therapy than spending the day feeling depressed
And alone. Good days and bad days come and go,
I just wish the lost days didn't happen so often.

Love

Some people say Love is about caring,
Some people say Love is about sharing,
I say Love is about them both. When
You Love someone, you care about all
Of the things that pertain to the one
That you Love. And when you Love
Someone, you share all of the things
That are important to the one that you
Love as well. It is both caring and
Sharing that make a relationship to
Be complete. Beyond the caring and
The sharing, you need to work together
At making Love a success. You go to
Dinner together, you go to movies
Together, you go shopping together,
You go on walks together, you spend
All of your free Tyme working at making
The relationship work. SomeTymes it
Is the simplest of things that you do for
The one that you Love that can make
The biggest difference in how you see
Your partner.

Lush

A man sits on his chair and he stares out the
Window at the big wide world. Feeling all
Alone, he thinks he's got nowhere else to go
And no one to turn to, so he turns to his one
Constant "friend," a bottle of liquor that's
Always been there for him when he's down.
He pours himself a drink. He feels the sting
As the whiskey hits his throat, his one
Reminder that soon the whiskey will be
There to answer his call for "company."
The liquor goes down easy as he is in need
Of companionship. Soon the booze is
Flowing and he remembers his first couple
Of Tymes he drank and how sick he got,
But not anymore. Now the drinks go down
Easier and easier. He remembers when he
Had a family all those years ago. He also
Remembers he had friends, real friends that
He went places with and did things with.
He remembers when he was younger how
Much more alive he felt in his twenty's and
Thirty's. Now in his seventy's, the years
Have all passed him by but he remembers
The constant friend he always had was
The liquor that he Loved so much more
Than his family and friends. Now the bottle
Is the only one left beside him...So he pours
Himself another and another until he falls
Asleep in the chair again...and again...
And again...

Mirror

When I look into your eyes, I see a mirror
Of myself, someone who is in Love. Though
Things don't always go the way that I plan,
I know that I Love you more than life itself.
With that being said, I want you to know
With the two of us working together at it,
We can be happy and live as one: one heart
One mind and one soul working together
To build a relationship that works for the
Both of us. Life isn't easy, but with the
Both of us working at it, we can accomplish
The goals we have set for ourselves. Little
By little and bit by bit we are becoming
More successful at reaching those goals.
Remember that things take Tyme to come
To fruition and nothing happens overnight,
But with the two of us intent on making
Our goals attainable, we can make it and
Slowly good things will happen for us.
I know that with you by my side, nothing
Is impossible and out of the realm of the
Possible.

My Best Friend

You're my best friend
You'll Love me when I'm old,
You're my best friend
You've got a heart of gold.

You're my best friend
You lift my spirits high,
You're my best friend
You encourage me to try.

You're my best friend
You take me out to eat,
You're my best friend
You're humor can't be beat.

You're my best friend
You hold me in your arms,
You're my best friend
You keep me safe from harm.

You're my best friend
You really rock my world,
You're my best friend
You're my favorite girl.

You're my best friend
You call me every day,
You're my best friend
You wash my fears away.

You're my best friend
You help me face my fears,
You're my best friend
You wipe away my tears.

My Childhood

As I look back on my childhood
I'm left here feeling sad,
As I look back on my memories
All I can feel is bad.

I never was a happy child
This I know is true,
I was all alone and crying
Now I'm here feeling blue.

No matter where I went
I never quite fit in,
I stood out like a sore thumb
I feel that way again.

Yes, my childhood was quite lonely
I felt that way each day,
My only consolation is that
Over Tyme my memories fade.

My Old Home Town

I went back to my old home town yesterday. I went
Back to see what I had been missing these past thirty
Years or so. Funny thing, when I went there, things
Hadn't really changed that much in all the Tyme that
I had been gone. Yes, the park where I grew up was
Still there, and except for new swings, it hadn't even
Changed a stitch since the last Tyme that I had been
Back there, oh, so many years ago. The homes seemed
The same except that they seemed awfully worn and
In need of repair. The old trail that I used to run on
Was still there and to my surprise, many of the places
That I had been employed as a teenager had been
Turned into more modern, useful things. My old
Church was still there, but the schools that I had
Attended had all been replaced with newer editions
Of themselves. My old house where I grew up was
Still there standing where it had been for over one
Hundred years. Funny how it seemed so many things
In my life had changed, but some of the things that I
had expected to be new and modern were really old
And in need of fixing. The one good thing I'd
Remembered were my family and friends, they were
All still there. They hadn't changed much, but just
Gotten older and I noticed the same of myself. I had
Not gotten older, just more refined and wiser. And
That was alright with me.

Next to Me

When you lie next to me I can feel your
Skin on mine as it gently warms mine
Own. The sight of you all stretched out
And sleeping helps me to relax because
I can feel your gentle breathing and I
Can feel your chest rising and falling
In tune with your soft breathing. I like
To feel your heartbeat next to mine as
It tells me that you are at ease, but more
Than this, I Love to see your face all
Relaxed as you sleep next to me. It tells
Me that you are comfortable and at ease
Enough in my presence to just drift off
To a place of sleep with me right by
Your side.

Nothing is Impossible

When the whole world seems to get me
Down, I know exactly what to do...I close
My eyes and I think of you and I don't
Feel alone anymore.

When I'm feeling sad and down, I just
Pretend that you're around. I close my
Eyes and I think of you and then I'm not
Sad anymore.

If I'm scared and full of fright and I feel
Like I can't make it through the night
I close my eyes and think of you and
Then I'm not scared anymore.

With you by my side, nothing is impossible.

Once Upon a Tyme

Once upon a Tyme we were friends
The kind to be there till the end,
But you went and found someone new
I'm feeling alone, what more can I do?

Guess we were not meant to be
You're really not who you seem,
Now I can't find my way back
Now it's just your Loving I lack.

Now I'm left here feeling half dead
Like so many things I've come to dread,
I wish that I knew a way to have all of
Your memories erased.

For now I'll have to just say goodbye
Though I'd rather have you here in my life,
No, nothing hurts more than to know
That this is the end of the road.

So now it's Tyme to just say goodbye
Still, I would give us one more try,
But it's Tyme to say goodbye once again
Enough of the deceit and lying my friend.

Once Upon a Tyme...#2

Once upon a Tyme back when
I woke up feeling down again,
I tried to get my mood on track
And fix the feelings that I lack,

I tried to get someone on the phone
Because I didn't want to feel alone,
I went to find something to eat
But nothing sounded good to me,

So I sat upon my purple chair
And tried to watch the T.V. there,
Then I tried next to go to bed
To rid the demons from my head,

But I couldn't get to sleep
Because my feelings were too deep,
No, nothing's going to change my mood
And get me back to feeling good,

So I tried to take a walk outside
But I just stayed inside and cried,
So I sat and cried all day
Trying to get my moods to sway,

I felt the tears run down my face
I hoped they would my mood erase,
I couldn't get my mood to change
And help my nerves to rearrange,

Yes, someTymes it's ok to cry
Until such moments pass me by.

One Day at a Tyme

When the days seem long and there seems
To be no hope in sight, I will get through
My days just one day at a Tyme. I need to
Not always focus on the bad and try to
Remember the parts of my day that have
Been successful, even when there has been
Just a portion of my day that has gone well.
I need to get through the day someTymes
By just focusing on a few minutes of the
Day that went right, even though it seems
Like the entire day was a bust. It sounds
So cliché to say it, but it truly is a way to
Survive when it seems like I'm carrying
The entire weight of the world on my
Shoulders. Just take it one day at a Tyme,
Minute by minute and hour by hour until
The day is through. I will take each day
Separately and by itself, just the way
They come…one day at a Tyme. Not
Worrying about the past and not obsessing
On the future…just one day at a Tyme.

One For the Two of Us

At the end of the show, no matter where we go
It always ends in two, no matter what we do,
Just two, just two, just one for me and one for you.

At the end of the morn, no matter how we're torn
It always ends in two, no matter what we do,
Just two, just two, just one for me and one for you.

At the end of the show, no matter where we go
It always ends in two, no matter what we do,
Just two, just two, just one for me and one for you.

At the end of the day, no matter what we say
It always ends in two, no matter what we do,
Just two, just two, just one for me and one for you.

At the end of the night, no matter wrong or right,
It always ends in two, no matter what we do,
Just two, just two, just one for me and one for you.

No matter where we go, no matter what we do,
At the end of what we do, it always ends in two,
Just two, just two, just one for me and one for you.

One Set of Hands

When I was younger, it seemed like I could
Make friends so easy and it seemed like the
Friends that I had were genuine. Somewhere
In my thirties, I stopped making friends in a
Snap and it was like I was pulling teeth to get
Any support from them. It was then that I
Realized that what I had were false friends
Who were just people who hung around me
For what they could get from me or what I
Could do for them. It took me a while to
Realize that I was being used for the things
I could provide for them. I realized that I
Had a few people who were my core group
Of friends, people that I could count on no
Matter what. They were the group of people
That I had chosen to keep around for support
and for emotional stability. There wasn't a
Lot of my real friends, but just enough to
Keep me company and be there for me when
I needed it most. A friend once said that you
Can count all your real friends on one set of
Hands...and it is the truth. The real friends
You can count on to be there aren't many, but
Just enough to be there when you really need
It and just enough to keep you happy...just
Enough.

Open Arms

At the end of the day, when I am weary,
I turn to you for support. When push
Comes to shove, I always know that I
Can count on you to be there. Through
Thick and through thin, you are the one
Who is there to greet me with open arms
And your affection. The days seem to
Get longer as Tyme goes by, but you are
My constant force for good. I know
That when I am feeling down or feeling
Sad you are always there with something
Nice to say that will cheer me up. On the
Days when things go alright, you are
Always there to share in the joy of a
Wonderful day just as much as the ones
That don't go well. With a smile, you can
Bring my mood to a better place, just by
Your being you.

Peace and Tranquility

Peace for me has always been when I am alone,
SomeTymes in my room and someTymes it's
Just a nice warm chair in the sun. Peace can
Be a warm sunny day, or a cool dreary day
Just watching it rain outside. SomeTymes I'm
At peace just listening to Mother Nature out-
Side, the wind whistling in the trees, watching
The animals as they scamper around. Some-
Tymes I'm at peace as I listen to the cold wind
Outside and I'm snuggling under a warm blanket
Just watching it snow. Peace isn't something
That comes easy for me. Much of the Tyme I
Am sad or unhappy or just miserably angry at
The world for being in such a mess. I've tried
So hard so hard to just let go and enjoy some
Quiet moments in my yard or just sitting in a
Park…but peace rarely seems to come to me.
I watch other people enjoy their lives doing
Everything from walking a dog to enjoying a
Drink out of doors. Peace is not a friend of
Mine and when peace and I finally cross paths
It is usually for a very short period of Tyme.
When I do finally come to be at peace I try to
Enjoy it for all that I can.

Picturesque

Take a picture and you'll be reminded
Of a moment lost in Tyme,
Take a moment and remember
That now you are all mine.

Each day with you is special
Each day is something new,
Each day I now am happy
Because I am with you.

Once when I was younger
I yearned for a Love so strong,
Now that I am older
You help me know where I belong.

We're a perfect pair of lovers
Whose Love is strong and true,
Each day with you is special
Because I belong to you.

We have a perfect relationship
Whose Love is strong and rare,
We are the perfect couple
Our Love shows that we care.

Pillar

We have been together for so long, so long, for so long.
When I think back about the changes we've been through
I can't help myself but fall in Love with you again. We
Have been through a battle or two, but we always come
Out stronger for it in the end. You are my pillar who
Helps me to get through it all. Standing tall or laying low
You are my rock who keeps me going through the good
Tymes and the bad...and I Love you for it. God knows
That there are Tymes when things got rough and we
Thought that it would end...but when the wars were over
We were always together, still holding on...holding on...
We were holding on for dear life. Now in the later years
We've grown so close and we both know that nothing
Will ever tear us apart. So now we just sit back just
Holding hands, both of us knowing that the best is yet
To come. Growing up and growing older, we were
Always meant to be, so just sit back and hold my heart
Closer than you ever have before...because no matter
Where we go and no matter what I do, I keep in my heart
These sweet thoughts of you.

Powerful Books

Whenever you feel that you're too wrapped up
In the stress of the world, let a book be your
Key to another world and another place in Tyme.
There's a sort of magic that exists between the
Reader and a good book that has the power to
Traverse you into another world or someone
Else's life that is so very magical. Think about
It, that book is merely paper and ink, but the
Way it moves you out of the hum drum you're
In is a very special thing. All too often people
Choose to watch a movie rather than read a
Novel. In a movie there is no imagination
Involved at all. It has all been visually made
And prepared for you. When you read a good
Book, the only limitations that exist to trans-
Port you into the writer's mind are the limits
Of the reader's own imagination. The other
Great thing about books is that you can put
Them down and pick them up again when you
Are ready to be moved again. Books can go
With you anywhere because they are portable.
The next Tyme you want an exciting adventure,
Let the pages of a book transport you to the
Worlds of limitless imaginations of your own
Mind.

Puddles

I was sitting back and remembering a Tyme
When I was young and playing with a small
Puppy named puddles that my grandmother
Had so appropriately named because where
Ever he went he left puddles on the ground.
He was a little guy that made me smile. All
I wanted to do was spend some Tyme running
Around and chasing each other as little kids
Will often do. I was remembering having to
Run from two roosters named Rudy and Reddy
That chased us all around the farm. It is funny
How much I so enjoyed her rustic place because
Of all of the room there was to play out of doors.
Helping grandpa to water the crops that grew
Was exciting because it never really felt like
We were doing chores. And spending Tyme
Together made me feel like those days would
Never end. But Tyme runs its course and
Things change and people leave us behind
Here to remember them. I wish I had told
Grandma and grandpa just how much I Loved
Them. I miss them terribly and wish I still
Had that big farm to run to when things get
Me down. But the one thing that they left
Me were some good memories to look back
On. I wish I had let them know how special
They made me feel when I had the chance.
Funny, somehow I think they always knew.

Quite the Little Lady

Once when I was lonely
I found a cat named Kaydee,
She became my dearest friend
She's quite the little lady.

She has golden eyes that shine
She's colored the black of night,
For when she rests upon me
She makes my dark days bright.

When she's feeling cold
She'll sit upon my lap,
I'll pet her then I'll brush her
And then she takes her nap.

And when she gets bored with life
She'll sit and start to play,
She likes to chase around her toys
She's chased my blues away.

There's something unique about her
She's become my dearest friend,
I think it's the way she smiles at me
She's helped my heart to mend.

Rabbit

I saw a baby rabbit in the yard. Tiny and
Vulnerable, just sitting there trying to
Survive. It got me thinking just how very
Lucky we as humans we really are. We
Take so many things for granted: because
We are humans we have a roof over our
Head to protect us from the wind, the rain
And the snow…protection from the heat
And cold. Being human, we don't have
To worry about being eaten by predators
Who would eats us for lunch or dinner.
Another thing we are privileged to have
Is food at our disposal, not hunting for
Three square meals a day. We just go
To the kitchen and make ourselves a
Meal when we are hungry. I wondered
How often that little rabbit gets to eat
Three meals a day and how far he has to
Go to find shelter so he can eat his meal
In peace. That tiny little bunny seemed
So scared of people. I often wondered
How many Tymes people try to kill him
For being a pest in their yards. The most
Serious of questions I had was just where
And how often that little guy can find
Something like water to drink when he
Gets thirsty. We as humans are very lucky
We have so many advantages over the other
Animals in our animal kingdom.

Sit Next to Me

Come sit next to me, we can talk we can
Hug and we can feel okay.
And though there is so much on my mind
I don't have much to say.

So I will hold you, yes I will hold you now
And we can speak of Love.
You're quiet, yes you are quiet and you're
As gentle as a dove.

So now we're lost, yes we're so lost, just
The two of us in Tyme.
And I now know, yes I now know that you
Are mine, all mine.

So now I reach out, yes, now I reach out for
Your hand to hold.
Because holding on for your affections never
Gets to feeling old.

So, now I reach out and kiss you, then I kiss
You once again.
Loving you is the greatest feeling because you
Are my greatest friend.

So Graceful

She sits gracefully upon my lap
As stares out the window there,
She sees the raindrops falling
Out on the tree limbs so bare.

SomeTymes she wishes she could run
Out of doors where she could be free,
Still she sits upon my lap in the afternoon
Still she spends her Tyme with me.

And as the Tyme passes us by
She grows tired and takes a nap,
She looks so small and curled up
As she dozes on my lap.

So we just sit and pass the Tyme of day
Just waiting for some better weather,
She just sits and purrs the day away
As we spend our day together.

So Grateful to You

When you whisper in my ear, that you Love me
Is all that I hear, and I'm grateful so I take a
Look at you and say, "I Love you so much too,"
And I do, I do , yes I do.

When you look into my eyes, you say with some
Surprise that you need me too. I stare back into
Your eyes and say, "I need you, yes I need you
Too." and I do, yes I do, I need you too.

When you take me by the hand, it just makes me
Feel so grand, and I hold your hand in mine, just
Saying all the Tyme that, "I long to have you by
My side." and I do, yes I do, yes I do too.

When you're laying by my side, it just makes me
Feel so right. And when you put your arms around
Me holding me tight, you tell me that "You feel so
Right and I long to never let you go." And all I can
Say is that "I Love you, too, yes, I do, yes, I do, I
Love you too."

So Much More...

You are the reason that I am here.
You brought me into this world
Oh, so many years ago. You have
Been my support system over the
Past four decades and you never
Stop the sharing of yourself. Your
Kind words make me feel better
When the world has gotten me
Down. You are always there for
Me when I need a shoulder to
Cry on. You tell the best stories
And always remind me how very
Lucky that I am to have such a
Wonderful family of support.
You bring me up when no one
Else can. Your voice is like a
Beacon of hope...strong for all
Who need it. When things don't
Go right, you are the voice of
Reason in the confusion. You
Are so much more than just a
Mother to me, you are truly my
Best friend and confidant. Thank
You for being the warm, wonderful
Person you always are. I Love you
So very much more than you'll
Ever know. I am so proud to be
Your son.

Something

Is there life beyond this place?
Something beyond this human race...
Something that lives beyond the stars...
Something beyond our Saturn and Mars...
Something that's born to make wars cease...
Something to help us live in peace...
Something that's smart with a wonderful brain...
Something to help us end all of our pain...
Something that will remind us it's o.k. to care...
Something that will remind us it's o.k. to share...
Something that will come down from the sky...
Something that will grant us just one more try...
Something to remind us to be a friend...
Something to help us until Tyme's end...
Something that's built and made of Love...
Something God made in the heaven's above.

Spend Every Moment With You

Chip away my heart of stone
I don't want to be alone,
I float on a river of tears
I don't want to face all my fears,

Whenever I feel this way
I just don't know what to say,
No, there's nothing I'd rather do
Than spend every moment with you.

I want to hold you in my arms
I want to keep you safe from harm,
You are the man of my dreams
I Love you more than it seems,

I just want to take it slow
I just wanted you to know,
Everything that I want to do
Is spend every moment with you.

I want to take you by the hand
I want to take a walk in the sand,
We've been so close from the start
I'll hold you near to my heart,

I just want to see your face
I want to keep you here in my space,
No, there's nothing I'd rather do
Than spend every moment with you.

Spring Rain

I just Love to take a walk out in the spring rain,
The plants are growing and the light is just barely
Showing through the clouds of gray. Cool drops
Fall on my skin and I welcome in the season, for
It is just another reason to celebrate the fact that
We are alive. Grasses grow and trees make leaves
And animals are all around so look alive. Let the
Rain come by and celebrate your life by jumping
In puddles and walking on through the light spring
Shower as it fills each day with life just one more
Tyme, so celebrate with me. Flowers drink up the
Drops of life giving, soul moving liquid that gives
Them life…so walk along in the cool clean air and
Celebrate life, for it is life that gives us life. Each
Day is another chance to move on and give us this
Wonderful state of grace

Still of the Night

Laying together in the still of the night, I can't
Help but think of you and all that you've come
To mean to me: my man my heart, we've been
Together from the start, we were always meant
To be. Now when the weather outside grows
Colder, I long to hold you closer...closer than
I've ever held you before. In the late of the
Night we sleep so right and hold on till the
Dawn's early light will wake us once again.
All through the day regardless of where we go
To, we will return at night to hold each other
Tight and share just a kiss or two. When the
Evening comes I know that we I would rather
Spend each night with you than spend even a
Single night alone. When the moonlight shines
Through the night and all the stars are at peace
I can't help but to feel the same way, too. But
All too soon the sun will rise and take you from
Me for just the day, but as the nightTyme returns
So do you my Love and once again you're in my
Arms once more. So sit and sleep my Loving friend,
I'm here until the dawn wakes us once again.

Summer Fun

You can do some fun things when it gets hot
Having fun doesn't have to cost a lot,
You can read a new book or a magazine
Or go and see a movie that you haven't seen,

Try going swimming at a swimming hole
Or you could catch fish with a fishing pole,
You can build a castle on the beach from sand
Or have fun running a lemonade stand,

Play a game of ball at a nearby park
Take in the fireworks when it gets dark,
You can enjoy just soaking up the sun
Or invite a friend to a walk or a run,

Go for a ride in a nice cool car
Have fun trying to count all the stars,
Take your skateboard down a great big hill
Try fixing dinner on a nice hot grill,

Have fun catching fireflies in the air
Enjoy some rides at the county fair,
Take your bike for a cruise down the lane
Enjoy a walk in the nice cool rain,

Go for a ride down a water slide
Take a motorcycle for a ride,
Have a rummage sale in your back yard
Or invite some friends to a game of cards,

Oh, those lazy days in the summer sun
You can stay cool while you still have fun.

Sunshine

Sunshine makes the sky look bright
Sunshine fills the day with light,
Sunshine helps the grass to grow,
Sunshine helps to melt the snow,
Sunshine grows the grapes on the vine,
Sunshine helps to make me feel fine,
Sunshine can chase away the blues,
Sunshine makes me feel renewed,
Sunshine moves without a sound,
Sunshine leaves shadows on the ground,
Sunshine chases the night away,
Sunshine I hope you'll always stay.

Take Another Look

When you're feeling lonely, when you're feeling sad
Take another look around you, then you won't feel bad.

Take another look around you, take another look and see
The one who's always been there is me.

When you're feel unhappy, when you're feeling down
Take another look around you, you know I'll be around

Take another look around you, take another look and see
The one who's always been there is me.

When you're feeling scared, when you're full of fright
Take another look around you, you know who'll make
Things right.

Take another look around you, take another look and see
The one who's always been there is me.

When you're feeling happy, when you're full of glee
Take another look around you, you know just where
I'll be.

Take another look around you, take another look and see
The one who's always been there is me.

When you're feeling out of sorts, when you're feeling bad
Take another look around you, you know I'll make you glad.

Take another look around you, take another look and see
The one who's always been there is ME.

That Girl

Once I knew the joy of a girl
One who made up my world.
She meant the world to me
She helped my heart to be free.

She knew the way I felt
She helped my cold heart to melt
She left and walked away
Now nothing feels the same.

Now nothing makes me feel fine
Now nothing leaves me sublime.
I wish I could go back in Tyme
I wish I could make her all mine.

But she belongs to someone new
Oh what more can I do.
I went and changed my world
Over the loss of that girl.

If I ever get a second chance
I'd give her Love and promise romance.
Nothing would ever change my world
Like the one I lost over that girl.

The Joy of Running

It starts with some warm up exercises, some
Stretches, some push ups and a few sit ups.
You stretch some more. You put on your
Running shoes and some light weight clothes
That fit loosely. Once you are nice and flexible
You walk outside and hit the pavement feet first.
Then you're off! You've got to remember to
Pace yourself so you don't get too winded until
You are done running. One…two…one…two
Your feet touch the ground and you bounce
Right back off of it. Left foot…right foot…
Left foot…right foot…now you've got that
Rhythm going and you've got to keep it up.
You stop thinking about the other things going
On in your life and focus on the breathing and
The foot work. You don't think about anything
But the rhythm you've got going on…step,
Bounce, step, bounce. No bills to pay, not a
Thing on your mind but keep on running…
And you do…you keep on running…You've
Made your mark by keeping track of the Tyme.
After 20 minutes you are nothing but a running
Machine. After 35 minutes you know that it is
Tyme to start slowing down. After 10 more
Minutes of slowing down you stop and you
Warm down. You look at yourself…you're
Covered in sweat so you do the right thing
And hit the showers you running beast. And
You do… yes, you do…yes, you do.

The Same Stars

When the sun goes down at night and
The moon rises up in the sky, I look up
And see all the stars that shine on the
Velvety black background and I make
A wish or two. When the moon begins
Her journey across the horizon, I can't
Help but stop and think of you and
Where you are tonight. Though we
Are far apart, we are both looking up
At the same stars and moon and wishing
You were here by my side so we could
Both share a kiss or two. Even though
The moon can't hear me I know she
Still knows how very much I wish we
Were still together tonight. I know
That she's sending down a smile for
The both of us. But until we can be
Together again, we'll just have to
Settle on wishing on the same stars
And moon for luck.

The Spell

We were just two little kids as I think back and I
Remember. We used to play outside in the daylight
Just holding hands. She was the first girl that I fell
In Love with at the tender age of five. Pink dresses
And a sailor suit, we were all dressed up and going
Nowhere, but she had a spell on me, oh, yes, she
Had a spell on me. Tea parties or just playing in the
Mud, it really didn't matter because we were two
Little kids in Love and we were the best of friends
As well. Drawing on the sidewalk or sharing a pan-
Cake or two…breakfast, lunch or dinner Tyme, we
Were together like two little peas in a pod. We would
Share all that we had and sometimes a kiss or two.
Julie, oh, Julie, you were the sweetest girl that I knew.
Tricycle races and going places, we were two little
Kids in Love…but then things changed when we had
To move away. But some things never do, I will
Never forget that spell you had on me…that spell
You had on me…that spell you had on me.

The Sun

When the sun shines down
From the big, big sky,
It makes me wish
That I could fly, fly, fly,

Up in the air
Is where I would go,
And wave to the people
So far down below,

I wish that I could
Be so intensely bright,
And so be able
To light up the night,

And then too
I'd light up the day,
And make the clouds
To fade away,

And I would help
The plants to grow,
And in the winter
I'd melt the snow,

I'd burn to keep
All that lives alive,
And help the entire planet
To grow and thrive,

Oh, what could be better
And be more fun,
Then to be the strong
And beautiful sun.

The Surreal Life

Oh, life isn't what it once seemed
I'm caught up in a really bad dream,
You were the one that I loved so,
You were the one that I Loved so.

So here's the way that I feel
Like nothing is really real,
It's only surreal, surreal, surreal.

I wish I could find a way
To turn back the Tyme on today,
I'd make everything fine,
I'd make my way back to the sublime.

So here's the way that I feel
Like nothing is really real,
It's only surreal, surreal, surreal.

Can't turn back and change the past,
I've got to live in the now at last,
I wish I could find a way,
To have your memory erased.

I'd do things another way,
I'd do things to show how I feel,
Like nothing is really real,
It's only surreal, surreal, surreal.

There Comes a Tyme...

There comes a Tyme in everybody's life
When they get to feeling down and out,
And when that happens you feel like
Your life has reached an end. It's then
That you have to make a decision about
What to do to remedy the situation, all I
Need to do is to turn to you and all that
Sadness slips away. I know that come
Hell or high water, you'll be there to
Support me and lift my spirits up where
They need to be. I know that even if my
Sadness hangs around for a while, you'll
Be there to help me make it through it
Until it is over. You alone can help me
To survive the incredibly low Tymes
When nothing else can raise my moods.
When I get to feeling angry at the world
There is only one thing that I can count
On to help me see through the upset that
Has gotten me mad and that's you. You
Are the one who helps me to see that the
Mood that I'm in is but a transitory state
Of feeling. You bring a calmness to me
That helps put the world back into a real
Perspective and realize that it won't last
Forever. You have the power to keep me
Grounded when I need it most and I am
Most thankful to you for that.

Thinking First of You

I start my day by thinking first of you
There's nothing in the world I'd rather do,
I turn to you and give you a big kiss
This takes me to a special place of bliss,

I think of you as I step out the door
I know I'll see you tonight some more,
I think about you all through out my day
Tonight we'll be together come what may,

I think of you through out my day and smile
It helps to make me happy for a while,
We can have dinner when we get back home
Then we will spend some special Tyme alone,

We can watch our favorite shows on the T.V.
While we are holding hands just you and me,
Then I'll think about the things you've said
And soon it will be Tyme to go to bed,

When we go to bed I will say a prayer
That in the morning you will still be there,
I'll start my day by thinking first of you
There's nothing in the world I'd rather do.

To Dad

SomeTymes when I'm all alone I get to thinking
About my father. And when I do, so many, many
Unanswered questions start to unfold. I wonder
If you're happy now that you've left this world
Behind. I wonder if you've found peace and
Tranquility wherever it is that you are. Often I
Think about the way life could have been for my
Family and myself, how things might have been,
And how things should have been. I know that
As a father you were never proud of me and the
Things that I have accomplished in my life. I
Wonder if you were ever proud, but too darned
Stubborn to say so. I also wonder why you spent
The greater portion of your life away from us,
Your family. Why did you ever make a family
And never bother to spend Tyme with us when
You were sober? What was it about life that
Made you have to hide your feelings in a bottle?
Were you sad as I I believe you were or were
You just too darned selfish to include us in your
Scheme of things? Now that you're far, far away
Do you ever regret the fact that you didn't include
Us more in your life? Did you find the contentment
And joy that you never found while you were alone
Here on earth? I can only say I hope you found what
You were looking for.

Together, You and Me

When you're feeling low,
When you feel you've nowhere else to go,
You can count on me,
Just take a look and see,
We were meant to be together, together, you and me.

So next Tyme that you're down,
Just take a look around,
You can count on me,
Just take a look and see,
We were meant to be together, together, you and me.

And when you feel a kiss,
Is something that you miss,
You can count on me,
Just take a look and see,
We were meant to be together, together, you and me.

Next Tyme you're feeling old,
And need a hand to hold,
You can count on me,
Take a look and see,
We were meant to be together, together, you and me.

When you feel you can't,
Remember that you can,
Darling look at me,
Then my Love you'll see,
We were meant to be together, together, you and me.

Treading Water

SomeTymes you can't keep your head above
Water, you feel like you're drowning. When
This happens, someTymes all you can do is
Tread water...not really swimming and not
Drowning but somewhere stuck in the middle
In limbo. I am quite familiar with this as
There are days when I can't seem to keep
Myself from going under and drowning in
My sorrows for the day. There are those days
That nothing you attempt goes right and you
Feel like you are going to lose your ability
To lose your cool. You don't want to make
A scene and start crying so you just tread
Water for what can seem like days, but it's
Just getting through the day. SomeTymes
When you're treading water, you feel like
You're going to run out of energy and find
Yourself going under. It's o.k. to tread water
From Tyme to Tyme, but what you need to
Remember is if you can't keep from going
Under and start crying that this is o.k. too.
SomeTymes the only thing you can do is
Let all your pain and anguish out of your
System and cry it all out. SomeTymes I
Find myself treading water for several days
In a row. This is hard to do because the
Sadness has to eventually be set free. If
You find that you can't hold it back any-
More, let it go free and go with it.

Until My Days Are Done

When I smile I think of you
There's nothing I would rather do,
You bring a smile to my face
Doubt disappears without a trace,

You, you are my closest friend
One who'll be there till the end,
So now you take me by the hand
And lead my heart across this land,

And no matter where we go
There's no one else I'd rather know,
You are the one I Love the most
You're the best from coast to coast,

And when you stop and smile at me
There's no one else I'd rather be,
Yes, you are the one I Love
God must have sent you from above,

So end my day now with a kiss
It sends me to a place of bliss,
Yes, now I know you are the one
I'll Love until my days are done.

Waiting

All alone I sit...waiting for the day to come
When all of my sins will be forgiven and I
Can move on with my life. Waiting, waiting,
Waiting for that day. Waiting...so patiently
Just wishing it would come sooner than later.
But you know what they say...careful what
You wish for, you just might get what you
Wished for you know? So now I'm stuck
Here in limbo, trapped between two worlds
That are constantly colliding with one another.
So now I just sit and dream away the days
Just dreaming of the day when we can for-
Give one another and move on forward with
Our lives. So I sit here waiting for it all to
Come to fruition and you and I will once
Again live as one...One...ONE.

War

I say a prayer to the man upstairs,
I pray that we will all get along
Someday...but it doesn't matter
How much I pray, or how often,
We just can't seem to all get along.
And so the wars continue, people
Fighting over territory, whose is
It anyway? And wars continue
Over religious freedom, who is
Right and who is wrong? And
The wars continue over political
Freedom, and so it goes, and so
It goes. And the wars continue
Over gold and greed, and still
The wars rage on and on. So
I pray to God when I settle into
Bed that perhaps tomorrow will
Be different than today. So we
Pray and we pray that maybe
Tomorrow will be different than
Today...and the wars rage on...
And the wars rage on...still the
Wars rage on...

When I'm Down

When I'm down and feeling blue,
When there's nothing that I can do
To really change the way that I feel,
When the depression seems so unreal,

I start to crumble and I start to cry,
I feel the teardrops fall from my eye,

When the world seems to be so unkind,
When I feel like I've lost my mind,
I'm feeling sad and I feel all alone,
I'm feeling like I've been beat to the bone,

I start to crumble and I start to cry,
I feel the teardrops fall from my eye,

I'm feeling down and I'm feeling no good,
Nothing ever seems to change my mood,
It's been a while since I felt well,
I can't shake of this mood from hell,

I start to crumble and I start to cry,
I feel the teardrops fall from my eye,

Because when I'm down and feeling sad,
I can't help it but I'm feeling so bad,
I try to call you but you're not around,
I fear the dark and I fear the sounds,

Yes, I start to crumble and I start to cry,
I feel the teardrops fall from my eye,
No good can come from a day like today,
And I can't change how I feel anyway.

While you Lay next to Me

While you lay next to me, I can watch you as you
Sleep. I can watch you as you breathe slowly in
And out, in and out, in and out. And as you slowly
Breathe, I can watch your body moving so slowly,
Ever so slowly. Every once in a while your eyes
Twitch just a very tiny bit. I wonder as I you do
Just what you are thinking of and just what you
Are dreaming of…could it be me? Me? Me? Or
Are you thinking special thoughts about the two
Of us together? I know that somewhere in that
Head of yours you are dreaming the night away.
Once in a while I lean over and kiss you on the
Forehead and as I do I can't help but take in that
Scent of you, yes, that wonderful scent of you.
As I do I get lost in that aroma of your hair and
The smell of your clothes. I take just a moment
To realize how much I Love to watch you sleeping
Here from a distance, from a distance, how I Love
To watch you from a distance while you lay next
To me.

With You

To Love you is to need you and to Love you
Is to want you and always to hold you…You
Take me by the hand and I am lost inside your
World of Love. I reach out for a hand to hold
And it is you that I reach out to hold whenever
It is that I am lonely. Your beautiful smile
Makes me relax and breathe easier in part I am
With you and it is where I feel safe and Loved.
I feel the touch of your skin against mine and I
Know just where I belong to be…with you my
One true Love with you. When you are near me
I get lost inside your world. I only want to get
A chance to spend my life with you. You are
The kind of Love that I can't get enough of.

With You By My Side

With you by my side I don't feel alone
Anymore. With you by my side I can
Make it through another day because
I know that you are there to encourage
Me. With you by my side I can feel
Brave again because I know you are
There to protect me. With you by my
Side I can stand tall again because I
Know that you are there to lift my
Spirits upwards. With you by my side
I can know Love again because you
Share your Love with me. With you
By my side I'm not angry anymore
Because you are there to calm the
Fire that upsets me so I can know
Peace again. Thank you for always
Being there for me.

Yes, I Do

There's nothing in my life I'd rather do
Than be the one who is always there for you,
I think about you my whole day long
And if I'm feeling down I sing this song,

You're the one who was made just for me
And in your arms is where I long to be,
When you're with me I Love to see you smile
It takes away my stress for just awhile,

Maybe we can walk over to the park
And we can stay there until it gets dark,
When we get there I will take your hand
Then we can make a castle in the sand,

Then we can take a walk down to the sea
What a Tyme we'll have, just you and me,
And when it gets late we can come back home
And spend the night just you and I alone,

When it gets late I'll stop and bow my head
A will say a prayer as we get into our bed,
When it is Tyme I will shut out the light
As I go to sleep and dream of you tonight.

Yes, It's You

You, you're the one I need, when I'm down indeed
It's you, yes it's you, yes it's you.
You're the one I crave when I'm feeling afraid
It's you, yes it's you, yes its you.
You're the one that comes to my rescue when I'm
In need of a real good friend.
You're the one who comes to my rescue when I feel
Like I've reached the end and I don't know which
Way to go. It's you, yes it's you, yes it's you.

You're the one I Love, when it's push come to shove
It's you, yes it's you, yes it's you.
You're the one I call when I'm headed for a fall
It's you, yes it's you, yes it's you.
You're the one that comes to my rescue when I'm
I'm in need of a real good friend.
You're the one who comes to my rescue when I feel
Like I've reached the end and I don't know which
Way to go. It's you, yes it's you , yes it's you.

And when I'm down and hope just can't be found
It's you, yes it's you, yes it's you.
And when Tymes get rough and things get tough
It's you, yes it's you, yes it's you.
You're the one who comes to my rescue when I'm
In need of a real good friend.
You're the one who comes to my rescue when I feel
Like I've reached the end and I don't know which
Way to go. It's you, yes it's you, yes it's you.
Yes it's you, yes it's you, yes, it's always YOU.

You Are the One

Take my hand and hold it gently as you look into
My eyes. When I gaze at yours feel a soft and
Carefree feeling that tells me you feel the same
Way that I do. Whisper to me how you're feeling
And I will do the same for you, for you are the
One that makes my heart to beat faster. Take me
Into your arms so I can feel the power of your
Love holding me fast and strong. Hold on tight
And never let me go. I am the one who Loves
You just as much as you do me. When you
Whisper in my ear that you Love me I get all
Caught up in the situation and can hold back any
More. I kiss you, I just kiss you and I find that
I am lost in this game of Love. When you kiss
Me too, I know our feelings are mutual and I lose
Track of Tyme and space. Hold me, kiss me and
Make me leave all of my doubts far behind me.
You are the one...the only one...that makes me
Feel alive and you do, Yes, You Do, YES, YOU DO.